What's Happening to O

Blue Heron Brothers Tel

by Ardith M. Schneider

CONTENTS

A portion of the proceeds from this book will be donated to the Environmental Learning Center in Vero Beach FL. www.discoverelc.org

WHAT THIS STORY IS ABOUT

What would two heron brothers do if they couldn't find fish - their favorite food? You might say, "They would move to another place." But Hugh and Harry Heron are dedicated to their home. Patient and inquisitive, they decide to fly, wade and just stand still in their statuesque way, observing their Indian River Lagoon environment to see what is happening.

Right away the brothers realize that the habitat for fish is not what it used to be. The sea grass has died, and many mangrove trees have been destroyed to make way for sea walls and more humans. As they analyze the areas of the lagoon, they see why pollution in the water has caused healthy habitats to disappear.

On they fly, exclaiming about the amazing views from inlet lighthouses and describing the devices that clean the canals leading to the Lagoon. As you can see from the IRL* map on the back cover of this book, the Lagoon waters are affected by the inlets, rivers and canals. You can also see how that strip of water is situated between the mainland and the barrier islands along the coast. The inlets flush saline ocean water into the Lagoon while more polluted fresh water flows in from the canals and rivers. Hugh, the older brother, explains why the Lagoon is brackish and, also, why it's not a river even though *river* is part of its name.

Hugh and Harry find out that the destructive process that has been going on is called *eutrophication* (see Glossary). Human activity has caused this overabundance of nutrients in bodies of water like the Lagoon. Who would have thought that too many nutrients could be a bad thing? However, the water gets clouded up by all the algae this produces, making oxygen for living creatures in short supply. The heron brothers get down to the business of showing some good things that are being done to test and improve water quality. At the end of the book the herons are happy that people really are concerned about what is going on under the shallow waters of the IRL. They are talking about it, shouting about it and taking steps to fix it.
READ ON TO MEET HUGH AND HARRY. Awk! Awk!

* Indian River Lagoon (referred to as IRL in this book)

FACT: Young herons are brownish-gray with a black cap. As they get older, they become bluish-gray.

Round Island Park, Vero Beach

FACT: Herons are called partial migrators because some migrate and others do not.

4   Round Island Park, Vero Beach

FACT: Herons can see very well at night because of many photoreceptors in their eyes.

FACT: The Lagoon is the nursery of the ocean, serving as a spawning ground for many fish. The IRL is also a key flyway for many migrating birds.

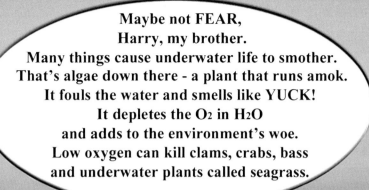

Maybe not FEAR,
Harry, my brother.
Many things cause underwater life to smother.
That's algae down there - a plant that runs amok.
It fouls the water and smells like YUCK!
It depletes the O_2 in H_2O
and adds to the environment's woe.
Low oxygen can kill clams, crabs, bass
and underwater plants called seagrass.

Is that why the water looks yucky like that?
There's dead seagrass here like a
floating mat.

FACT: H_2O is the chemical formula for water, and O_2 is the oxygen that is dissolved in it
(so important to marine animals). Seagrass is one of the most critical habitats of the IRL.

Merrill P. Barber Bridge, Vero Beach

FACT: The prop roots of the red mangrove provide a nursery area for young fish. After the protein-rich leaves fall into the water, they start to decay, providing food for lagoon creatures.

Round Island Park, Vero Beach

FACT: The green tops of the red mangroves are seen in the foreground. The black mangrove excretes salt from the brackish water through its leaves, while the red mangove removes salt using its roots.

FACT: The grapes attract birds, squirrels and other mammals. People can eat the grapes and often make jelly from them.

John's Island, Vero Beach

11

FACT: Besides natural islands like Pelican Island, there are over 137 small islands created in the 1950s by channel dredging. These are called Spoil Islands.

White Pelicans on Pelican Island, North Vero Beach

12

FACT: The five inlets from the north of the Lagoon to the south are: Ponce de Leon, Sebastian, Fort Pierce, St. Lucie and Jupiter (see map on back cover).

13

Sebastian Inlet Bridge

With these spectacles I can see for miles.
At this height
the Atlantic Ocean is an incredible sight.
This Ponce Lighthouse gives such a view
and we didn't have to climb 213 steps.
Whew!

Right behind me is the
beginning of the Indian River Lagoon
which we know isn't really a river at all.
It has no direction of flow as I recall,
but 156 miles of Lagoon is a long haul.
Squaaawk!

FACT: This inlet is a natural opening in the barrier islands along the coast. The inlet was named for Ponce de Leon, a Spanish explorer who first set foot in Florida in the early 1500s.

View from Ponce Lighthouse

FACT: The Fort Pierce Inlet is one of the man-made inlets to the Lagoon.
Boats and bathers must be aware of the strong currents in the outflow here.

Fort Pierce Inlet from the beach 15 at Fort Pierce Inlet State Park

FACT: Two man-made jetties (structures extending into the ocean to protect the harbor) were added to this natural inlet in 1922.

Jupiter Inlet Lighthouse

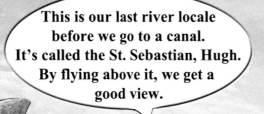

This is our last river locale
before we go to a canal.
It's called the St. Sebastian, Hugh.
By flying above it, we get a
good view.

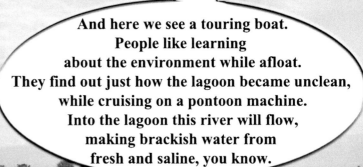

And here we see a touring boat.
People like learning
about the environment while afloat.
They find out just how the lagoon became unclean,
while cruising on a pontoon machine.
Into the lagoon this river will flow,
making brackish water from
fresh and saline, you know.

FACT: This river is part of a preserve that has now grown to encompass more than 35 square miles. The State of Florida and many local land trusts buy land to preserve creature habitats.

FACT: In one year Pollution Control Main in Vero Beach removed 637 tons of debris from our Lagoon waters. See ircstormwater.com for more information.

19   PC Main, Airport Road, Vero Beach

Merrill P. Barber Bridge (above)

FACT: If the freshwater plants had not been removed by Pollution Control Main, they would die in the brackish lagoon and create muck which can kill seagrass.

FACT: The algae is growing on a huge sloping concrete mat, that has water from the canal flowing over it. The dissolved nutrients in the water are food for the algae, so as the water flows down the mat the algae removes the disolved nutrients from the water. Every so often the algae is harvested. Then it regrows and continues to remove the nutrients.

FACT: Buffer zones maintain water quality, serving as filters for pollutants and runoff from adjacent land. Beemats (after the last name of the inventor) can be pulled in to shore for replanting.

Lagoon-side pond at The Moorings Yacht and Country Club, Vero Beach

22

Yes, Hugh,
there are 24 of these buoys surrounding this field.
So the seagrass cannot only grow but be healed.

This buoy marks a project that's really first class.
It's all about preserving and growing seagrass.
Even I know seagrass is the base of the food chain
and something we should work to sustain.

FACT: Seagrass zones like this one provide support for many local
fish, food for manatees and spawning areas for many species.

FACT: The empty shells attract free-floating oyster larvae. When the larvae are old enough to attach, they are called spat. One adult oyster can filter up to 50 gallons of water a day.

Beach on the Lagoon

FACT: There is a network of LOBOs (Land/Ocean Biogeochemical Observatories) in the IRL. They measure real-time, accurate water quality data through an interactive website.

FACT: The importance of devices like the LOBOs and Kilroys cannot be underestimated as they provide factual water quality information from various locations in real time.

Vero Beach City Marina

Hugh, I know you don't like to talk about waste.
But it's something that just has to be faced.
Stormwater runoff into the Lagoon comes from
many things which can be traced.

So true, Harry.
This is a culvert for stormwater discharges.
As it goes along, the water overflow enlarges.
Everything on the ground that's strewn
could eventually end up in the Lagoon!
That goes for fertilizer, septic tank seepage
and doggie poop.
That can really make the Lagoon a
nitrate soup.

FACT: With instruments like the LOBO and Kilroy, many chemicals and bacteria can be tracked
coming into the Lagoon. Pet waste, especially, contains fecal coliform bacteria which is bad for humans.

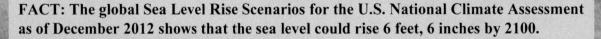

FACT: The global Sea Level Rise Scenarios for the U.S. National Climate Assessment as of December 2012 shows that the sea level could rise 6 feet, 6 inches by 2100.

28

FACT: The largest source of greenhouse gasses over the last 150 years in the United States is from burning fossil fuels for electricity, heat and transportation.

SOME THINGS THAT YOU CAN DO TO HELP OUR LAGOON

1. Just like Harry Heron, LEARN all you can about the environment and pollution.
2. Tell others about what you have learned - SPREAD THE WORD.
3. Be careful what you flush down the toilet - not paper towels, medicines, toxic waste.
4. Conserve your water use to lessen septic seeping. Ask your parents if they have the septic system pumped out every 3 to 5 years.
5. Pick up after your pets, and wherever you see plastic pick it up and dispose of it properly. Birds, fish, turtles and dolphins (even herons) can get caught up in it.
6. Urge your parents to reduce the turf in your yard. Use native plants which require less water and fertilizer.
7. Help clean your yard. Don't let plastic, oil, grass clippings and garbage run off your property.
8. Volunteer for environmental efforts! There's just not enough money to do everything.

FACT: REDUCE, REUSE and RECYCLE - in that order. The first one is the most difficult. Buy less, use less and select products that won't go into a landfill.

Photo Credit: Susan Webb   30   Wabasso Bridge, Vero Beach

GLOSSARY

algae - A freshwater or saltwater single or multi-cellular plant that has no roots, stems or leaves.

alma mater - Latin for "nourishing mother," school or college.

barrier island - Land form along the coast that is parallel to the mainland. First line of defense against a tidal surge.

detritus - Decomposed organic material not caused by erosion.

ecosystem - A complex network of living things functioning together in their environment.

estuary - A coastal water body, like a lagoon, where the ocean, river or canal waters merge.

eutrophication - A process where excessive nutrients (nitrates and phosphates) stimulate the growth of algae to the extent that it depletes oxygen killing marine life.

fecal coliform bacteria - A bacteria found in the feces of warm-blooded animals, including humans.

food chain - See illustration below.

habitat - The environment where an organism can live and grow.

inlet - A narrow water passage through a barrier island.

lagoon - A shallow body of brackish water separated from the ocean by a barrier island.

larvae and spat - Fertilized oyster eggs become larvae and these larvae attach themselves to another shell or suitable surface and become spat (pictured at left).

nutrients - Nourishment for plants: nitrogen, and potassiam.

photoreceptors - A group of cells specialized to receive light.

pollution - The introduction of contaminants into the environment that cause negative change.

pontoon - Floatation device, ususally on the inderside of a flat-bottomed boat.

rain garden - A shallow cavity planted with deep-rooted native plants to absorb runoff. (see illustration p. 32.)

septic system - Sewage disposal tank in which waste material is decomposed by bacteria.

spawning - The process of eggs and sperm being released into water.

toxin - A poison of animal or plant origin.

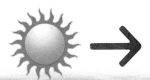 

ALL CANALS
FLORIDA
NO Trash!
INDIAN RIVER LAGOON
LEAD TO LAGOON

ACKNOWLEDGEMENTS

Cynthia Callander and Susann Pezetti, Vero Beach Book Center
Paul Dritenbas, Conservationist (Oysters, Seagrass)
Dennis Hanisak, Research Professor, Harbor Branch Oceanographic Institute
Brian LaPointe, Research Professor, FAU Harbor Branch Oceanographic Institute
Erin Lomax, Education Department, Ocean Discovery Center, Harbor Branch
Keith McCully, Stormwater Engineer, Stormwater Division, Indian River County
Charles Paxton, NOAA Science and Operations Officer, National Weather Service
Robin Pelensky, Landscape Architect, Judy and Bob Prosser, background advisors
Nyla Pipes, Director One Florida Foundation
Joel Rockwell, generous friend with a boat
Eve Samples - TCPalm editor, Susan Webb, Photographer
Heather Stapleton, Education Director, Environmental Learning Center, Vero Beach
Craig Weyandt, Naturalist, Moorings Yacht and Country Club, Vero Beach
Cindy Willson, Educator Lagoon Life
Camille Yates, Development Director, Environmental Learning Center, Vero Beach

THANKS TO THE ABOVE FOR THEIR EXPERTISE, CLARIFICATION AND PHOTOS

SPECIAL THANKS TO MY EDITORS
Helen Jankoski, James Morris and Liz Sayre for their help with grammar, ideas and style!

REFERENCES

Websites: www.beemats.com, www.discoverelc.org (Environmental Learning Center), www.fau.edu/jboi/meh (Harbor Branch,Marine Ecosystem Health), www.fmel.ifas.ufl.edu (seagrass), www.ircgov.com (Indian River County), www.ircstormwater.com (stormwater division), www.sjrwmd.com (St. Johns River Management), www.stateparks.com,www.water.epa.gov (Indian River Lagoon PDF Water).

JUST ANOTHER GOOD IDEA TO PROTECT THE LAGOON

stormwater

rain garden soil mix

Rain Gardens are becoming more popular in Florida.

Plants for rain gardens do not need fertilizer and can absorb runoff and pollutants.

Robin Pelensky

clean water

32